To the common people.

GUIDE TO HUMAN RIGHTS

ABIRLAL MUKHOPADHYAY

ISBN 978-1-68487-833-8

Contents

Preface

This foundation course is developed for one and each who wants to learn human rights and their functions. Securing human rights is a collective responsibility and all people should have little or more knowledge on it. In this course, we would cover the definitions, meanings, history and evolution, characteristics, functions and importance of human rights.

About The Author

Abirlal Mukherjee (2000 - Present)

Abirlal Mukhopadhyay was born in West Bengal on 21 August, 2000 and spent his early childhood in Jharkhand. After returning home, he had his higher secondary from his village school and passed being the block topper the same year. From Bankura Christian College he completed his bachelor's degree in English Literature.And M.A in English from Bankura University. At the age of twenty one Abirlal has written more than ten books and published in hundreds of anthologies both in English and Bengali. India Book of Records appreciates Abirlal Mukhopadhyay for publishing five interesting books at the early age of twenty years nine months. In 2021, Abirlal Mukhopadhyay was awarded with India Prime Author Award by Foxclues for his book The Living Corpses, Limelight Award as the Best Author of the year 2021 by The Opus Coliseum, Star Golden Award by Suman Art Theatre for the contribution in the field of literature, RCrit Author Award by RCrit Review for his book The Cry From the Fire. Abirlal Mukhopadhyay is marked as the Best Young Promising Author 2021 and awarded with Influential Indian's Award by The Crazy Tales.

To name a few books of Abirlal: The Cry From The Fire, The Rough Sketches of Life, The Living Corpses, Heart to Art, Syntax, The Days She Dreamt For and other books. His short stories include The Fishmonger, The Ticket Collector, A Birthday Cake, Freak, Me too, A Freedom Fighter, Satyriasis, A Plague. His fictions and poems have a close study of human emotions. Their innermost desires are well expressed in some of his poems: 'Can't', 'Survive', 'Never', 'Deciduous', 'Baltimore Oriole'. He took part in several national and international exhibitions of art. Abirlal worked as a co-writer and invited author for various magazines and publishing houses. Some of them are: Blue Hill Publication, The Opus Coliseum, Flairs and Glairs. Abirlal Mukhopadhyay is also appointed the same year as a board member of the Indian Human Rights Organisation West Bengal. Later got promoted as the Additional Chief Secretary of Indian Human Rights Organization.

The early writings of Abirlal Mukhopadhyay were in Bengali. From his secondary school days, he started contributing in different anthologies in Bengali. It was when he was in college, he started publishing his works in English. Unspoken, unsung human pain and emotions, declining morality, unheard voices get their prominent place in the works of Abirlal. In the book The Living Corpses the girl named Baliel stood as a representative of the abused teens in the workplace and everywhere.

The Cry From the Fire
The Cry From the Fire explores the abusive male characters who hold power and drink the life of others for pleasure. The tribal life is portrayed in The Cry From the Fire. One evening in the forest a boat came with a white man and a big black bag. The man with a black jacket entered the forest with the bag and came back barehanded. Varsha noticed everything from a distance. The boat disappeared. But what was there in the bag!

A widow of twenty-five, Varsha, lived at the periphery of a little village amidst the forest. And the two white babies lived with her, Wherefrom she got them!

Sukla was the elder son of the witch, Raka. After the death of the witch her second son, Sukhdev decided to marry but at the marriage night Varsha mistakenly drank the sanctified water and the marriage got suspended by the priest for the next lunar eclipse. An old woman who came to Varsha's cottage also died that night. Villagers suspected her as devilish. The atmosphere became heavy...

At midnight Bashu with two other men entered her cottage and after a few hours, they fired the cottage with the widow of twenty-five...

Her screaming, the pain of the two children who called Varsha 'mother' made the night darker than others...

But who helped the children to escape from the village!

The Living Corpses

The Living Corpses tells a strange story. In a specific corner with a fixed spine, Mita sometimes could hear a voice from the air when she looked with blink-less eyes at the yellow dots of light coming from the forest office. She was a social worker and a content writer. There are seven chapters in the book, Mita is the only character who links the different incidents. There are people: seventeen-year-old Belial who lost her parents in the same year and got physically abused by two, Pandit who couldn't reach his family to see his little child's dead body as he worked miles away and it was lockdown. Sundar, Sahib and some other characters are introduced in Book One. Though the story is one fiction but inspired by some real incidents from the year 2020.

The Days She Dreamt For

In the book The Days She Dreamt For we see a girl who migrated to another district of West Bengal due to a hydrometeorological disaster with her poor father, had the vision to see possibility in everything, she failed multiple times, her love left her without even a prior information, her father died but she knew how to innovate, her vision led her long, her start up became a giant, and she became able to get her love back and to gift her lover a piece of land on lunar surface.

The Rough Sketches of Life
This book is a collection of rough sketches of life, sadness, anger, pleasure, pain, disappointment, and the emotions one enjoys or suffers. A blend of quote and poem, a handbook with life.

Mystery, suspense and complexity of plot make each of his stories more relishing.

Reference links and Press Release:

Hindustan Times: https://www.hindustantimes.com/brand-post/top-educationists-and-authors-honoured-by-foxclues-india-prime-awards-for-2021-101627043063471.html

RCrit Review: https://www.rcritreviews.com/abirlal-mukhopadhyay/

Spot Latest: https://spotlatest.com/news/foxclues-india-top-100-educationists-researchers-and-authors-awarded-with-india-prime-awards/3703/

CHAPTER I

Abbreviations

ACHR - American Convention on Human Rights

AHRD - ASEAN Human Rights Declaration

AICHR - ASEAN Intergovernmental Commission on Human Rights

CAT - Committee against Torture

CED - Committee on Enforced Disappearances

CEDAW - Convention on Elimination of All Forms of Discrimination against Women

CERD - International Convention on the Elimination of All Forms of Racial Discrimination

CERD - Committee on Economic, Social and Cultural Rights

CMW - Committee on Protection of the Rights of All Migrant Workers and Members of Their Families

COHRE - Centre on Housing Rights and Evictions

CRC - Convention on Rights of the Child / Committee on the Rights of Children

CRPD - Convention on the Rights of Persons with Disabilities / Committee on the Rights of Persons with Disabilities

ECHR - European Convention for the Protection of Human Rights and Fundamental Freedom

ECRI - European Commission against Racism and Intolerance

ECHR - European Court of Human Rights

HRC - Human Rights Council

IACHR - Inter-American Commission on Human Rights

ICC - International Criminal Court

ICCPR - International Covenant on Civil and Political Rights

ICERD - International Covenant on the elimination of All Forms of Racial Discrimination

ICESCR - International Covenant on Economic, Social and Cultural Rights

ICJ - International Court of Justice

ILO - International Labour Organisation
MDGs - Millennium Development Goals
NGO - Non-government Organisation
NHRIs - National Human Rights Institutions
OHCHR - Office of the United Nations High Commissioner for Human Rights
UDHR - Universal Declaration of Human Rights
UNDP - United Nations Development Programme
UN-Habitat - United Nations Human Settlements Programme
UNICEF - United Nations Children's Fund
WTO - World Trade Organization

CHAPTER II

Introduction to Human rights

Human- A member of the homo-sapiens species; a man, a woman, child or a person in general.
Rights - Things to which you are entitled or allowed, the freedom that is guaranteed.

"Where, after all, do universal human rights begin? In small places, close to home -- so close and so small that they cannot be seen on any maps of the world. [...] Unless these rights have meaning there, they have little meaning anywhere. Without concerted citizen action to uphold them close to home, we shall look in vain for progress in the larger world."
- Eleanor Roosevelt

Definitions:

The only way to define something is to find out its characteristics and tie them together in one or more aphoristic sentences. Before we try to define human rights, we must have a bird's eye view of what other organizations, people, and scholars have found out. Read the following definitions:

Human rights mean the right relating to life, liberty, equality, and dignity of individuals guaranteed by the constitution or embodied in international covenants and enforced by courts in India.
- Section (2) of The Protection of Human Rights Act 1993

Human rights are foreign to no culture and native to all nations: they are universal.

- Kofi A. Annan, former Secretary-General of UN

Human rights as a claim to something of crucial importance for human life.
- Susan Okin

All human rights are universal, indivisible and interdependent and interrelated. The international community must treat human rights globally in a fair and equal manner, on the same footing, and with the same emphasis.
- Vienna Declaration and Programme of Action, World Conference on Human Rights, 1993

"Men are born and remain free and equal in rights. Social distinctions can be founded only on the common utility."
-French Declaration of the Rights of Man and the Citizen (1789)

Everyone has the right to freedom of opinion and expression: this right includes freedom to hold opinions without interference and to seek, receive and impart information and ideas through any media and regardless of frontiers - Article 19 of The Universal Declaration of Human Rights

Human Rights are common for all human beings on the earth and they are regardless of sex, family, creed, colour, language, religion, national, state, race, ethnicity, varnas, castes, place and etc. Human Rights Day is observed every year on 10 December — the day the United Nations General Assembly adopted, in 1948, the Universal Declaration of Human Rights (UDHR).

Characteristics of Human Rights

- Human rights are rights that every human being has by virtue of his or her human dignity.
- Human rights are the sum of individual and collective rights laid down in State Constitutions and international law.
- Human rights are manifold.
- Human rights are universal irrespective of race, colour, sex, ethnic or social origin, religion, language, nationality, age, sexual orientation, disability or any other distinguishing characteristic.
- Human rights are inalienable
- Human rights are indivisible and interdependent

Democracy, parliaments and human rights

''As an ideal, democracy aims essentially to preserve and promote the dignity and fundamental rights of the individual, to achieve social justice, foster the economic and social development of the community, strengthen the cohesion of society and enhance national tranquillity, as well as to create a climate that is favourable for international peace. As a form of government, democracy is the best way of achieving these objectives: it is also the only political system that has the capacity for self-correction.'' Inter-Parliamentary Union, Universal Declaration on Democracy, Cairo, September 1997, paragraph 3

Democracy today is not a mere set of procedural rules for the political power exercise, but a way of preserving and promoting the dignity of the person. In the Universal Declaration on Democracy adopted in 1997, democracy and human rights are inseparable.

Basic Human Rights in UDHR
The 30 basic human rights mentioned in the articles of the Universal Declaration of Human Rights are followings:

The Universal Declaration of Human Rights (abbreviated)
Article 1 Right to Equality
Article 2 Freedom from Discrimination
Article 3 Right to Life, Liberty, Personal Security
Article 4 Freedom from Slavery
Article 5 Freedom from Torture and Degrading Treatment
Article 6 Right to Recognition as a Person before the Law
Article 7 Right to Equality before the Law
Article 8 Right to Remedy by Competent Tribunal
Article 9 Freedom from Arbitrary Arrest and Exile
Article 10 Right to Fair Public Hearing
Article 11 Right to be Considered Innocent until Proven Guilty
Article 12 Freedom from Interference with Privacy, Family, Home and Correspondence
Article 13 Right to Free Movement in and out of the Country
Article 14 Right to Asylum in other Countries from Persecution
Article 15 Right to a Nationality and the Freedom to Change It
Article 16 Right to Marriage and Family
Article 17 Right to Own Property
Article 18 Freedom of Belief and Religion
Article 19 Freedom of Opinion and Information
Article 20 Right of Peaceful Assembly and Association
Article 21 Right to Participate in Government and Free Elections
Article 22 Right to Social Security
Article 23 Right to Desirable Work and to Join Trade Unions
Article 24 Right to Rest and Leisure
Article 25 Right to Adequate Living Standard
Article 26 Right to Education
Article 27 Right to Participate in the Cultural Life of Community
Article 28 Right to a Social Order that Articulates this Document
Article 29 Community Duties Essential to Free and Full Development
Article 30 Freedom from State or Personal Interference in the above Rights

CHAPTER III

History, Evaluation and Objectives of Human Rights

History and Evaluation of Human Rights

The Cyrus Cylinder (539 B.C)

In 539 B.C., the armies of Cyrus the Great, the first king of ancient Persia, conquered the city of Babylon. But it was his next actions that marked a major advance for Man. He freed the slaves, declared that all people had the right to choose their religion, and established racial equality. These and other decrees were recorded on a baked-clay cylinder in the Akkadian language with a cuneiform script. The script is now known today as the Cyrus Cylinder, this ancient record has now been recognized as the world's first charter of human rights. It is translated into all six official languages of the United Nations and its provisions parallel the first four Articles of the Universal Declaration of Human Rights.

The Magna Carta (1215)

The Magna Carta, or "Great Charter," was arguably the most significant early influence on the extensive historical process that led to the rule of constitutional law today in the English-speaking world.

In 1215, after King John of England violated several ancient laws and customs by which England had been governed, his subjects forced him to sign the Magna Carta, which enumerates what later came to be thought of as human rights. Among them was the right of the church to be free from governmental interference, the rights of all free citizens to own and inherit property and to be protected from excessive taxes. It established the right of widows who owned property to choose not to remarry and established principles of due process and equality before the law. It also contained provisions forbidding bribery and official misconduct.

Widely viewed as one of the most important legal documents in the development of modern democracy, the Magna Carta was a crucial turning point in the struggle to establish freedom.

Petition of Right (1628)

The next recorded milestone in the development of human rights, produced in 1628 by the English Parliament and sent to Charles I as a statement of civil liberties. Refusal by Parliament to finance the king's unpopular foreign policy had caused his government to exercise forced loans and to quarter troops in subjects' houses as an economic measure. Arbitrary arrest and imprisonment practice for opposing these policies had produced in Parliament a violent hostility to Charles and George Villiers, the Duke of Buckingham. The Petition of Right, initiated by Sir Edward Coke, was based upon earlier statutes and charters and asserted four main principles:

(1) No taxes may be levied without the consent of Parliament

(2) No subject may be imprisoned without cause shown (reaffirmation of the right of habeas corpus)

(3) No soldiers may be quartered upon the citizenry, and

(4) Martial law may not be used in times of peace.

The English Bill of Rights (1689)

The English Bill of Rights (1689) is responsible for the constitutional monarchy in England, meaning the king or queen acts as head of state but his or her powers are limited by law. Under this system, the monarchy couldn't rule without the consent of Parliament, and the people were given individual rights. In the United Kingdom, the Bill of Rights is further accompanied by Magna Carta, the Petition of Right, the Habeas Corpus Act 1679 and the Parliament Acts 1911 and 1949 as some of the basic documents of the uncodified British constitution.

The Virginia Declaration of Rights (1776)

The Declaration was adopted unanimously by the Fifth Virginia Convention at Williamsburg, Virginia on June 12, 1776, as a separate document from the Constitution of Virginia which was later adopted on June 29, 1776. George Mason was the principal author of the Virginia Declaration of Rights. The Declaration consists of sixteen articles on the subject of which rights "pertain to [the people of Virginia] ... as the basis and foundation of Government."

The Declaration can be considered the first modern Constitutional protection of individual rights for citizens of North America. It rejected the notion of privileged political classes or hereditary offices such as the members of Parliament and House of Lords described in the English Bill of Rights.

The Virginia Declaration of Rights was drafted in 1776 to proclaim the inherent rights of men, including the right to reform or abolish "inadequate" government. It influenced several later documents, including the United States Declaration of Independence (1776) and the United States Bill of Rights (1789).

US Declaration of Independence (1776)

On July 4, 1776, the United States Congress approved the Declaration of Independence. Its primary author, Thomas Jefferson, wrote the Declaration as a formal explanation of why Congress had voted on July 2 to declare independence from Great Britain, more than a year after the outbreak of the American Revolutionary War, and as a statement announcing that the thirteen American colonies were no longer a part of the British Empire. Congress issued the Declaration of Independence in several forms. It was initially published as a printed broadsheet that was widely distributed and read to the public.

Philosophically, the Declaration stressed two themes: individual rights and the right to revolution. These ideas became widely held by Americans and spread internationally as well, influencing in particular the French Revolution.

The Constitution of the USA (1787) and Bill of Rights (1791)

Written during the summer of 1787 in Philadelphia, the Constitution of the United States of America is the fundamental law of the US federal system of government and the landmark document. It is the oldest written national constitution in use and defines the principal organs of government and their jurisdictions and the basic rights of citizens. The first ten amendments to the Constitution—the Bill of Rights—came into effect on December 15, 1791, limiting the powers of the federal government of the United States and protecting the rights of all citizens, residents and visitors in American territory.

The Bill of Rights protects freedom of speech, freedom of religion, the right to keep and bear arms, the freedom of assembly and the freedom to petition. It also prohibits unreasonable search and seizure, cruel and unusual punishment and compelled self-incrimination. Among the legal protections it affords, the Bill of Rights prohibits Congress from making any law respecting the establishment of religion and prohibits the federal government from depriving any person of life, liberty or property without due process of law. In federal criminal cases, it requires indictment by a grand jury for any capital offence, or infamous crime guarantees a speedy public trial with an impartial jury in the district in which the crime occurred and prohibits double jeopardy.

French Declaration of the Rights of Man and the Citizen (1789)

In 1789 the people of France brought about the abolishment of the absolute monarchy and set the stage for the establishment of the first French Republic. Just six weeks after the storming of the Bastille, and barely three weeks after the abolition of feudalism, the Declaration of the Rights of Man and the Citizen (French: La Déclaration des Droits de l'Homme et du Citoyen) was adopted by the National Constituent Assembly as the first step toward writing a constitution for the Republic of France.

The Declaration proclaims that all citizens are to be guaranteed the rights of "liberty, property, security, and resistance to oppression." It argues that the need for law derives from the fact that "...the exercise of the natural rights of each man has only those borders which assure other members of the society the enjoyment of these same rights." Thus, the Declaration sees law as an "expression of the general will," intended to promote this equality of rights and to forbid "only actions harmful to the society."

The First Geneva Convention (1864)

In 1864, sixteen European countries and several American states attended a conference in Geneva, at the invitation of the Swiss Federal Council, on the initiative of the Geneva Committee. The diplomatic conference was held to adopt a convention for the treatment of wounded soldiers in combat.

The main principles laid down in the Convention and maintained by the later Geneva Conventions provided for the obligation to extend care without discrimination to wounded and sick military personnel and respect for and marking medical personnel transports and equipment with the distinctive sign of the red cross on a white background.

The Universal Declaration of Human Rights (1948)

The Universal Declaration was adopted by the General Assembly as UN Resolution A/RES/217(III)[A] on 10 December 1948 in Palais de Chaillot, Paris. December 10, the anniversary of the adoption of the Universal Declaration, is celebrated annually as World Human Rights Day or International Human Rights Day.

The Universal Declaration of Human Rights (UDHR) is an international document adopted by the United Nations General Assembly that enshrines the rights and freedoms of all human beings. It was accepted by the General Assembly as Resolution 217 during its third session on 10 December 1948 at the Palais de Chaillot in Paris, France. Of the 58 members of the United Nations at the time, 48 voted in favour, none against, eight abstained, and two did not vote.

It directly inspired the development of international human rights law and was the first step in the formulation of the International Bill of Human Rights, which was completed in 1966 and came into force in 1976.

During World War II, the Allies—known formally as the United Nations—adopted as their basic war aims the Four Freedoms: freedom of speech, freedom of religion, freedom from fear, and freedom from want. Towards the end of the war, the United Nations Charter was debated, drafted, and ratified to reaffirm "faith in fundamental human rights, and dignity and worth of the human person" and commit all member states to promote "universal respect for, and observance of, human rights and fundamental freedoms for all without distinction as to race, sex, language, or religion". In 1999, the Guinness Book of Records described the Declaration as the world's "Most Translated Document", with 298 translations; the record was once again certified a decade later when the text reached 370 different languages and dialects.

The International Covenant on Civil and Political Rights (1966)

The International Covenant on Civil and Political Rights (ICCPR) is a multilateral treaty adopted by United Nations General Assembly Resolution 2200A (XXI) on 16 December 1966, and in force from 23 March 1976 following Article 49 of the covenant. The ICCPR is part of the International Bill of Human Rights, along with the International Covenant on Economic, Social and Cultural Rights (ICESCR) and the Universal Declaration of Human Rights (UDHR). The ICCPR is monitored by the United Nations Human Rights Committee (a separate body to the United Nations Human Rights Council), which reviews regular reports of States parties on how the rights are being implemented.

The Covenant follows the structure of the UDHR and ICESCR, with a preamble and fifty-three articles, divided into six parts.

Human Rights Calendar

27 January- Holocaust Memorial Day
January 27 marks the anniversary of the liberation of Auschwitz-Birkenau, the largest Nazi death camp. In 2005, the United Nations General Assembly designated this day as International Holocaust Remembrance Day (IHRD), to honour the victims of the Nazi era.

2nd Tuesday of February - Safer Internet Day
Safer Internet Day is organised by Insafe to promote safer and more responsible use of online technology and mobile phones, especially amongst children and young people.

12 February - Red Hand Day
Organisations supporting the Global Red Hand Campaign to stop the use of child soldiers include Human Rights Watch, Amnesty International, Youth Red Cross Germany, Terre des Hommes and Plan International.

21 February - International Mother Language Day
Since 1999 UNESCO has promoted this day to encourage broad and international commitment to promoting multilingualism and linguistic diversity, including the safeguarding of endangered languages.

8 March - International Women's Day
International Women's Day (8 March) is a global day celebrating the economic, political and social achievements of women past, present and future. The first IWD was in 1911. The UN began observing International Women's day in 1975.

12 March - World Day Against Cyber Censorship
World Day Against Cyber Censorship was observed on 12 March

2009 at the request of Reporter Without Borders and Amnesty International.

18 March - First Parliamentary Election with Universal Suffrage in Europe
This was in Finland in 1917.

21 March - World Poetry Day (Declared by UNESCO in 1999)
The purpose of the day is to promote the reading, writing, publishing and teaching of poetry.

21 March - International Day for the Elimination of Racial Discrimination On this day, in 1960, police opened fire and killed 69 people at a peaceful demonstration in Sharpeville, South Africa, against the apartheid "pass laws". Proclaiming the Day in 1966, the General Assembly called on the international community to redouble its efforts to eliminate all forms of racial discrimination.

22 March - World Day for Water
First formally proposed in Agenda 21 of the 1992 United Nations Conference on Environment and Development (UNCED) in Rio de Janeiro, Brazil. The observance began in 1993 and aims at promoting awareness of the extent to which water resource development contributes to economic productivity and social well-being.

23 March - World Meteorological Day
The World Meteorological Organization (WMO). Its work of weather forecasting is important in providing food security, water resources and transport.

24 March - World Tuberculosis Day
On this day in 1882, Dr Robert Koch presented his discovery of the TB bacillus to a group of doctors in Berlin. It was proclaimed an official day in 1992 by WHO.

2nd Tuesday in April - European Equal Pay Day
Proclaimed by BPW Europe (Business and Professional Women).

7 April - World Health Day
Proclamée en 1950 par l'Organisation Mondiale de la santé pour sensibiliser aux souffrances inacceptables de la mère et de l'enfant et aux efforts de tous nécessaires pour préserver la vie et la santé.

23 April - World Book and Copyright Day
By celebrating this Day UNESCO seeks to promote reading, publishing and the protection of intellectual property through copyright. The Day was first celebrated in 1995. Also known as World Book Day.

24 April - Armenian Genocide Remembrance Day
24 April 1915 marks the beginning of the genocide when the Ottoman government arrested and murdered hundreds of Armenian intellectuals and community leaders in Constantinople (Istanbul). It is estimated that 1.5 million Armenians were killed in a series of massacres and starvation that followed.

28 April - World Day for Health and Safety at Work
Declared by the International Labour Organization (ILO).

1 May - International Workers Day
Also known as "May Day". It is a celebration of the International Labour Movement.

2nd Saturday in May - World Fair Trade Day
Declared by the World Fair Trade Organisation.

3 May - World Press Freedom Day
Declared by UNESCO in 1993 to promote press freedom in the world and to recognise that a free, pluralistic and independent press

is an essential component of any democratic society.

5 May - Europe Day (Council of Europe)
An annual celebration of peace and unity in Europe. There are two separate designations of Europe Day: 5 May for the Council of Europe and 9 May for the European Union.

8 May - World Red Cross and Red Crescent Day
World Red Cross Day remembers and recognises the efforts of the National Red Cross and Red Crescent Societies worldwide.

8-9 May - Remembrance and Reconciliation for Those Who Lost Their Lives During the
Second World War
Declared in 2004 by the United Nations General Assembly to pay tribute to all those who lost their lives in the Second World War.

15 May - International Day of Families
Declared in 1993 by the United Nations General Assembly to increase awareness of family issues.

17 May - The International Day Against Homophobia and Transphobia
UNAID Joint United Nations Programme on HIV/AIDS. Co-ordinated by the Paris based "IDAHO Committee".

17 May - World Information Society Day
Proclaimed by the UN in 2005 to raise global awareness of societal changes brought about by the Internet and new technologies. It also aims to help reduce the Digital divide.

21 May - World Anti-Terrorism Day
World Anti-Terrorism Day is to oppose all forms of terrorism and violence. It was initiated in India because "thousands of youth are lured into the folds of terrorist camps and organizations each year."

21 May - World Day for Cultural Diversity for Dialogue and Development
Proclaimed in 2002 by the UN to protect cultural diversity as a means of achieving prosperity, sustainable development and global peaceful coexistence.

22 May - International Day for Biological Diversity
Proclaimed in 2000 by the UN General Assembly for the promotion of biodiversity issues. The Day was previously observed on 29 December.

26 May - World Challenge Day
Organised each year by TAFISA (The Association for International Sport for All). Communities from around the world compete to motivate as many people as possible to be physically active.

28 May - European Neighbours Day
Sponsored by the Council of Europe. The aim is that cities and social housing organisations strengthen local communities by encouraging neighbourhood parties and other similar events.

29 May - International Day of United Nations Peacekeepers
Designated in 2002 by the UN to pay tribute to all the men and women who have served in UN peacekeeping operations for their high level of professionalism, dedication and courage, and to honour the memory of those who have lost their lives in the cause of peace.

31 May - World No-Tobacco Day
Started in 1987 by the WHO to encourage 24 hours of abstinence from all forms of tobacco to draw global attention to the widespread use of tobacco use and the health risks.

4 June - International Day of Innocent Children

Victims of Aggression Commemorated since 1982 to acknowledge and remind people of the suffering of many children victims of physical, mental and emotional abuse and of the need to protect the rights of children.

5 June - World Environment Day
Established in 1972 by the UN General Assembly to deepen public awareness of the need to preserve and enhance the environment.

12 June - World Day Against Child Labour
The International Labour Organization launched the first World Day Against Child Labour in 2002.

17 June - World Day to Combat Desertification and Drought
Proclaimed in 1995 by the UN to promote awareness of the need for international cooperation to combat desertification and the effects of drought, including implementation of the Convention to Combat Desertification.

20 June - World Refugee Day
Proclaimed in 2000 by the General Assembly to mark the 50th anniversary of the 1951 Convention relating to the Status of Refugees.

23 June - United Nations Public Service Day
Designated by the UN to highlight the contribution of public service in the development process.

26 June - International Day against Drug Abuse and Illicit Trafficking
The General Assembly in 1987 decided to observe this day to strengthen action and cooperation to achieve the goal of an international society free of drug abuse.

26 June - United Nations International Day in Support of Victims of

Torture
Proclaimed in 1997 by the UN, the day aims at the eradication of torture and the effective functioning of the 1984 Convention against Torture and Other Cruel, Inhuman or Degrading Treatment or Punishment. The day was first observed on 26 June 1987.

1st Saturday, July - International Day of Co-operatives Proclaimed in 1992 by the UN General Assembly.
The date marks the centenary of the International Co-operative Alliance recognising that co-operatives are an indispensable factor in development.

11 July - World Population Day
Proclaimed in 1989 by the United Nations

Objectives of human rights

- To protect human beings
- To develop individual self-respect
- To value human dignity
- To promote respect, understanding and appreciation of diversity
- To promote democracy, social justice and friendship among people and nature

CHAPTER IV

Kinds of Human Rights

Civil and Political Rights

- Right to life
- Freedom from torture and cruel, inhuman or degrading treatment or punishment
- Freedom from slavery, servitude and forced labour
- Right to liberty and security of person
- Right of detained persons to be treated with humanity
- Freedom of movement
- Right to a fair trial
- Prohibition of retroactive criminal laws
- Right to recognition as a person before the law
- Right to privacy
- Freedom of thought, conscience and religion
- Freedom of opinion and expression
- Prohibition of propaganda for war and of incitement to national, racial or religious hatred
- Freedom of assembly
- Freedom of association
- Right to marry and found a family
- Right to take part in the conduct of public affairs, vote, be elected and have access to public office

Economic and social and cultural rights

- Right to work
- Right to just and favourable conditions of work
- Right to form and join trade unions
- Right to social security

- Protection of the family
- Right to an adequate standard of living, including adequate food, clothing
- and housing
- Right to health
- Right to education

Collective Rights

- Right of peoples to:
- Self-determination
- Development
- Free use of their wealth and natural resources
- Peace
- A healthy environment
- Rights of national, ethnic, religious and linguistic minorities
- Rights of indigenous peoples

CHAPTER V

International Human Rights Instruments

Treaties

- International Covenant on Civil and Political Rights (ICCPR: adopted in 1966: entry into force in 1976)
- Optional Protocol to the ICCPR (OP-ICCPR; adoption in 1966; entry into force in 1976); Second Optional Protocol to the ICCPR aiming at the abolition of the death penalty (adoption in 1989);
- International Covenant on Economic, Social and Cultural Rights (ICESCR; adoption in 1966; entry into force in 1976);
- Optional Protocol to the ICESCR (OP-ICESCR; adoption in 2008; entry into force in 2013);
- International Convention on the Elimination of All Forms of Racial Discrimination (CERD; adoption in 1965; entry into force in 1969);
- Convention on the Elimination of All Forms of Discrimination against Women (CEDAW; adoption in 1979; entry into force in 1981);
- Optional Protocol to CEDAW (adoption in 1999; entry into force in 2000);
- Convention against Torture and Other Cruel, Inhuman or Degrading Treatment or
- Punishment (CAT; adoption in 1984; entry into force in 1987);
- Optional Protocol to CAT (OPCAT; adoption in 2002; entry into force in 2006);

- Convention on the Rights of the Child (CRC; adoption in 1989; entry into force in 1990);
- Optional Protocols to CRC on the involvement of children in armed conflict and on the sale of children, child prostitution and child pornography (adoption in 2000; entry into force in 2002);
- Optional Protocol to CRC on a communications procedure (adoption in 2011; entry into force in 2014);
- International Convention on the Protection of the Rights of All Migrant Workers and
- Members of Their Families (known as the Migrant Workers Convention; ICRMW; adoption in 1990; entry into force in 2003);
- Convention on the Rights of Persons with Disabilities (CRPD; adoption in 2006; entry into force in 2008);
- Optional Protocol to CRPD (adoption in 2006; entry into force 2008);
- International Convention for the Protection of All Persons from Enforced
- Disappearance (CED; adoption in 2006; entry into force in 2010)

United Nations Human Rights Treaty Monitoring Bodies
• Human Rights Committee;
• Committee on Economic, Social and Cultural Rights (CESCR-Committee);
• Committee on the Elimination of Racial Discrimination (CERD-Committee);
• Committee on the Elimination of Discrimination against Women (CEDAW-Committee);
• Committee against Torture (CAT-Committee);
Subcommittee on the Prevention of Torture and other Cruel, Inhuman or Degrading
Treatment or Punishment (SPT);
• Committee on the Rights of the Child (CRC-Committee);
• Committee on the Protection of the Rights of All Migrant Workers

and Members of
Their Families (CMW-Committee);
• Committee on the Rights of Persons with Disabilities (CRPD-Committee);
• Committee on Enforced Disappearances (CED-Committee).

CHAPTER VI

Three State Human Rights Obligations

25

Three State Human Rights Obligations

Introduction

Obligation is an act or course of action to which a person is morally or legally bound. states are the primary duty bearers of human rights obligations. The states have also a duty to provide a remedy at the domestic level for human rights violations. International human rights treaties and customary law impose three obligations on states: the duty to respect, the duty to protect, the duty to fulfil

The State's Obligation to respect, protect and fulfil

Right to life

Respect: The police shall not intentionally take the life of a suspect to prevent his or her escape.

Protect: Life-threatening attacks by an individual against other persons

(attempted homicide) shall be crimes carrying appropriate penalties under domestic criminal law. The police shall duly investigate such crimes to bring the perpetrators to justice.

Fulfil: The authorities shall take legislative and administrative measures to progressively reduce child mortality and other types of mortality whose underlying causes can be combated.

Prohibition of torture or cruel, inhuman or degrading treatment or punishment

Respect: The police shall not use torture in questioning detainees.

Protect: The authorities shall take legislative and other measures against domestic violence.

Fulfil: The authorities shall train police officers in acceptable methods of questioning.

Right to vote

Respect: The authorities shall not interfere with the voting procedure and shall respect the election results.

Protect: The authorities shall organize voting by secret ballot to preclude threats by persons in power (such as politicians, heads of clan or family or employers).

Fulfil: The authorities shall organize free and fair elections and ensure that as many citizens as possible can vote.

Right to education

Respect: The authorities shall respect the liberty of parents to choose schools for their children.

Protect: The authorities shall ensure that third parties, including parents, do not prevent girls from going to school.

Fulfil: The authorities shall take positive measures to ensure that education is culturally appropriate for minorities and indigenous peoples, and of good quality for all.

Right to health

Respect: The authorities shall not restrict the right to health (inter alia through forced sterilization or medical experimentation).

Protect: Female genital mutilation shall be prohibited and eradicated.

Fulfil: An adequate number of hospitals and other public healthcare facilities shall provide services equally accessible to all.

Right to food

Respect: The authorities shall refrain from any measures that would prevent access to adequate food (for instance, arbitrary eviction from land).

Protect: The authorities shall adopt laws or take other measures to prevent powerful people or organizations from violating the right to food

(such as a company polluting the water supply or a landowner evicting peasants).

Fulfil: The authorities shall implement policies – such as agrarian reform – to ensure the population's access to adequate food and the capacity of vulnerable groups to feed themselves.

Responsibilities of the state to protect

- The right to an effective remedy
- The principle of progressive realization
- The right to recourse to an international or regional human rights mechanism
- The right to reparation of harm suffered
- Remedies for violation of economic, social and cultural rights

CHAPTER VII

Human Rights in India

Our country was one of the original signatories to the International Covenant on Civil and Political Rights. The Indian State is obliged to guarantee certain civil liberties, which are specified in Part III of the Constitution of India. fundamental rights enshrined in Part III of the Constitution have emerged from the doctrine of natural rights. Fundamental Rights are the modern name for what has been traditionally known as Natural Rights. These rights are called the Fundamental Rights of the Indian citizen. These may be further subdivided into personal, social, cultural and economic rights. Such rights may also be called legal rights because it is guaranteed by the law of the land.

The development of such constitutionally guaranteed fundamental human rights in India was inspired by historical examples such as England's of Rights (1689), the United States of Rights (approved on 17 September 1787, final ratification on 15 December 1791) and France's Declaration of the Rights of Man (created during the revolution of 1789, and ratified on 26 August 1789). These rights are included in the constitution because they are considered essential for the development of the personality of every individual and to preserve human dignity. The first demand for fundamental rights came in the form of the "Constitution of India Bill, in 1895. Also popularly known as the Swaraj Bill 1895, it was written during the emergence of Indian nationalism and increasingly vocal demands by Indians for self-government. It talked about freedom of speech, right to privacy, right to franchise, etc. Part-III of the Indian constitution is known as the Magna Carta of the Indian Constitution. These rights are called fundamental rights because they are justifiable.

Some of the salient features of Fundamental Rights include:

FRs are protected and guaranteed by the constitution.

FRs are NOT sacrosanct or absolute: in the sense that the parliament can curtail them or put reasonable restrictions for a fixed period. However, the court has the power to review the reasonability of the restrictions.

FRs are justiciable: The constitution allows the person to move directly to the Supreme Court for the reinforcement of his fundamental right as and when they are violated or restricted.

Suspension of Fundamental Rights: All the Fundamental Rights are suspended during National Emergencies except the rights guaranteed under Articles 20 and 21.

Restriction of Fundamental Rights: The Fundamental Rights can be restricted during military rule in any particular area.

Important Articles Related To Fundamental Rights

Article 12: Defines The State

Article 12 of the Indian Constitution defines The State as:

The Government and Parliament of India, the Government and legislatures of the states, all local authorities and other authorities in India or under the control of the Government of India.

Article 13: Defines Laws Inconsistent with or In derogation of Fundamental Rights

Article 13 of the Indian Constitution states that:

All laws in force in the territory of India immediately before the commencement of this Constitution, in so far as they are inconsistent with the provisions of this part, shall, to the extent of such inconsistency, be void.

The State shall not make any law which takes away or abridges the rights conferred by this Part and any law made in contravention of this clause shall, to the extent of the contravention, be void. In this article, unless the context otherwise required, – (a) "law" includes any Ordinance, order, bye-law, rule, regulation, notification, custom or usage having in the territory of India the force of law; (b)"laws in force" includes laws passed or made by a Legislature or other competent authority in the territory of India before the commencement of this Constitution and not previously repealed, notwithstanding that any such law or any part thereof may not be then in operation either at all or in particular areas.

Nothing in this article shall apply to any amendment of this Constitution made under article 368.

Classification of Rights in India

ENUMERATION OF POLITICAL AND CIVIL FUNDAMENTAL RIGHTS UNDER THE CONSTITUTION OF INDIA

The political and civil rights are termed as 'Fundamental Rights' and enshrined in Part-III of the Indian Constitution which includes the following rights:—

(1) Right to equality - Articles 14, 15 and 16.

(2) Right to six freedoms - Article 19.

(a) Freedom of speech and expression.

(b) Freedom to assemble peacefully and without arms.

(c) Freedom to form associations or unions.

(d) Freedom to move freely throughout the Territory of India.

(e) Freedom to reside and settle in any part of the territory of India.

(f) Freedom to practise any profession or carry on any occupation, trade or business.

(3) Right to life and personal liberty - Articles 20, 21 and 22.

(4) Right to freedom of religion - Articles 25, 26, 27 and 28.

(5) Cultural and educational rights - Articles 29 and 30.

(6) Right to property - Article 31. (The 44th amendment has deleted this right and re-enacted it in Article 300 A, as a constitutional right).

(7) Right against exploitation - Articles 23 and 24.

(8) Right to Constitutional remedies - Article 32.

ENUMERATION OF CULTURAL, SOCIAL AND ECONOMIC RIGHTS UNDER THE DIRECTIVE PRINCIPLES OF THE

CONSTITUTION OF INDIA

Part-IV of the Indian Constitution detailing 'Directive Principles of State Policy lays down the following rights. The socialist and welfare precepts have particularly been incorporated in Article 39 of the Constitution.

(1) Right to adequate means of livelihood - Article 39 (a).

(2) Right against economic exploitation - Article 39 (e). The health and strength of both sexes and tender age of children are not abused and are not forced by economic necessity to enter avocations unsuited to their age or strength.

(3) Right to both sexes to equal pay for equal work - Article 39(d).

(4) Right to work - Article 41.

(5) Right to leisure and rest - Article 41.

(6) Right to public assistance in case of unemployment, old age sickness (Social Security) - Article 41.

Part IV of the Constitution also incorporates the Directive Principles of economic and social justice and certain ideals which the State should strive to achieve. Article 38 directs the State to bring about the welfare of the people by securing and protecting effectively a social order where justice, social, political and economic shall inform all the institutions of national life.

(7) It directs the State to create conditions where there will be no concentration of wealth and means of production to the common detriment and where the ownership and control of the material resources of the community are so distributed as best to sub-serve the common good. [Article 39 (b) and (c)].

Further, the Directive Principles are provided in the Articles of the Constitution mentioned below:

(8) Article 42 - Just and human conditions of work and maternity leave.

(9) Article 43 - Mandatory Payment of living wages etc. to workers.

(10) Article 44 - Uniform Civil Code.

(11) Article 45 - Free and Compulsory Education.

(12) Article 46 - Promotion of educational and economic interests of scheduled castes, scheduled tribes and other weaker sections.

(13) Article 47 - Duty of the State to raise the level of nutrition and the Standard of living and to improve public health.

(14) Article 48 - Organisation of agriculture and animal husbandry.

(15) Article 49 - Protection of monuments and places and objects of national importance.

(16) Article 50 - Separation of Judiciary from Executive.

(17) Article 51 - Promotion of international peace and security.

By 42nd Amendment of the Constitution, three more Articles were added therein:

(18) Article 43A - Participation of workers in the management of industries.

(19) Article 39A - Equitable justice and free legal aid.

(20) Article 48A - Protection and improvement of environment and safeguarding of forests and wildlife.

These additions by amendments are unexceptional.

Thus, a broad statement of the eminent scholar, K. Subba Rao, may be aptly acceded to: "What American and other highly developed democratic countries have achieved through judicial decision and pragmatism have been crystallized, embodied and improved upon by the Indian Constitution. (K. Subba Rao, Enforcement of Basic Human Rights in Law and the Commonwealth, 73).

The Protection of Human Rights Act, 1993; ACT NO. 10 OF 1994 [8th January 1994.] & National and State Human Rights Commission
(Select Sections)

An Act to provide for the constitution of a National Human Rights Commission, State Human Rights Commissions in States and Human Rights Courts for better protection of human rights and matters connected therewith or incidental thereto.

(1) The Central Government shall constitute a body to be known as the National Human Rights Commission to exercise the powers conferred upon and to perform the functions assigned to, it under this Act.

(2) The Commission shall consist of—

(a) a Chairperson who has been a Chief Justice of the Supreme Court;

(b) one Member who is, or has been, a Judge of the Supreme Court;

(c) one Member who is, or has been, the Chief Justice of a High Court;

(d) two Members to be appointed from amongst persons knowing of, or practical experience in, matters relating to human rights.

(3) The Chairperson of the National Commission for Minorities, 1[The National Commission for the Scheduled Castes, the National Commission for the Scheduled Tribes] and the National Commission for Women shall be deemed to be Members of the Commission for the discharge of functions specified in clauses (b) to (j) of section 12.

(4) There shall be a Secretary-General who shall be the Chief Executive Officer of the Commission and shall exercise such powers and discharge such functions of the Commission 2[(except judicial functions and the power to make regulations under section 40B) as may be delegated to him by the Commission or the Chairperson, as the case may be].

(5) The headquarters of the Commission shall be at Delhi and the Commission may, with the previous approval of the Central Government, establish offices at other places in India.

12. Functions of the Commission.—The Commission shall perform all or any of the following functions, namely:—

(a) inquire, suo-motu or on a petition presented to it by a victim or any person on his behalf 1[or on a direction or order of any court], into complaint of—

(i) violation of human rights or abetment thereof; or

(ii) negligence in the prevention of such violation, by a public servant;

(b) intervene in any proceeding involving any allegation of violation of human rights pending before a court with the approval of such court; 2[(c) visit, notwithstanding anything contained in any other law for the time being in force, any jail or other institution under the control of the State Government, where persons are detained or lodged for purposes of treatment, reformation or protection, for the study of the living conditions of the inmates thereof and make recommendations thereon to the Government;] 2[(c) visit, notwithstanding anything contained in any other law for the time being in force, any jail or other institution under the control of the State Government, where persons are detained or lodged for purposes of treatment, reformation or protection, for the study of the living conditions of the inmates thereof and make recommendations thereon to the Government;]"

(d) review the safeguards provided by or under the Constitution or any law for the time being in force for the protection of human rights and recommend measures for their effective implementation;

(e) review the factors, including acts of terrorism, that inhibit the enjoyment of human rights and recommend appropriate remedial measures;

(f) study treaties and other international instruments on human rights and make recommendations for their effective implementation;

(g) undertake and promote research in the field of human rights;

(h) spread human rights literacy among various sections of society and promote awareness of the safeguards available for the protection of these rights through publications, the media, seminars and other available means;

(i) encourage the efforts of non-governmental organisations and institutions working in the field of human rights;

(j) such other functions as it may consider necessary for the promotion of human rights.

13. Powers relating to inquiries.—

(1) The Commission shall, while inquiring into complaints under this Act, have all the powers of a civil court trying a suit under the Code of Civil Procedure, 1908, and in particular in respect of the following matters, namely:—

(a) summoning and enforcing the attendance of witnesses and examining them on oath;

(b) discovery and production of any document;

(c) receiving evidence on affidavits;

(d) requisitioning any public record or copy thereof from any court or office;

(e) issuing commissions for the examination of witnesses or documents;

(f) any other matter which may be prescribed.

(2) The Commission shall have the power to require any person, subject to any privilege which may be claimed by that person under any law for the time being in force, to furnish information on such points or matters as, in the opinion of the Commission, may be useful for, or relevant to, the subject matter of the inquiry and any person so required shall be deemed to be legally bound to furnish such information within the meaning of section 176 and section 177 of the Indian Penal Code.

(3) The Commission or any other officer, not below the rank of a Gazetted Officer, specially authorised in this behalf by the Commission may enter any building or place where the Commission has reason to believe that any document relating to the subject matter of the inquiry may be found, and may seize any such document or take extracts or copies therefrom subject to the provisions of section 100 of the Code of Criminal Procedure, 1973, in so far as it may be applicable.

(4) The Commission shall be deemed to be a civil court and when any offence as is described in section 175, section 178, section 179, section 180 or section 228 of the Indian Penal Code is committed in the view or presence of the Commission, the Commission may, after recording the facts constituting the offence and the statement of the accused as provided for in the Code of Criminal Procedure, 1973, forward the case to a Magistrate having jurisdiction to try the same and the Magistrate to whom any such case is forwarded shall proceed to hear the complaint against the accused as if the case has been forwarded to him under section 346 of the Code of Criminal

Procedure, 1973.

(5) Every proceeding before the Commission shall be deemed to be a judicial proceeding within the meaning of sections 193 and 228, and for the purposes of section 196, of the Indian Penal Code, and the Commission shall be deemed to be a civil court for all the purposes of section 195 and Chapter XXVI of the Code of Criminal Procedure, 1973. 1[(6) Where the Commission considers it necessary or expedient so to do, it may, by order, transfer any complaint filed or pending before it to the State Commission of the State from which the complaint arises, for disposal in accordance with the provisions of this Act: Provided that no such complaint shall be transferred unless the same is one respecting which the State Commission has jurisdiction to entertain the same.

(7) Every complaint transferred under sub-section (6) shall be dealt with and disposed of by the State Commission as if it were a complaint initially filed before it.]

14. Investigation.—

(1) The Commission may, for the purpose of conducting any investigation pertaining to the inquiry, utilise the services of any officer or investigation agency of the Central Government or any State Government with the concurrence of the Central Government or the State Government, as the case may be.

(2) For the purpose of investigating into any matter pertaining to the inquiry, any officer or agency whose services are utilised under sub-section (1) may, subject to the direction and control of the Commission,—

(a) summon and enforce the attendance of any person and examine him;

(b) require the discovery and production of any document; and

(c) requisition any public record or copy thereof from any office.

(3) The provisions of section 15 shall apply in relation to any statement made by a person before any officer or agency whose services are utilised under sub-section (1) as they apply in relation to any statement made by a person in the course of giving evidence

before the Commission.

(4) The officer or agency whose services are utilised under sub-section (1) shall investigate into any matter pertaining to the inquiry and submit a report thereon to the Commission within such period as may be specified by the Commission in this behalf.

(5) The Commission shall satisfy itself about the correctness of the facts stated and the conclusion, if any, arrived at in the report submitted to it under sub-section (4) and for this purpose the Commission may make such inquiry (including the examination of the person or persons who conducted or assisted in the investigation) as it thinks fit.

15. Statement made by persons to the Commission.—No statement made by a person in the course of giving evidence before the Commission shall subject him to, or be used against him in, any civil or criminal proceeding except a prosecution for giving false evidence by such statement: Provided that the statement—

(a) is made in reply to the question which he is required by the Commission to answer; or

(b) is relevant to the subject matter of the inquiry.

16. Persons likely to be prejudicially affected to be heard.—If, at any stage of the inquiry, the Commission—

(a) considers it necessary to inquire into the conduct of any person; or

(b) is of the opinion that the reputation of any person is likely to be prejudicially affected by the inquiry, it shall give to the person a reasonable opportunity of being heard in the inquiry and to produce evidence in his defence: Provided that nothing in this section shall apply where the credit of a witness is being impeached.

17. Inquiry into complaints.—The Commission while inquiring into the complaints of violations of human rights may—

(i) call for the information or report from the Central Government or any State Government or any other authority or organisation subordinate thereto within such time as may be specified by it: Provided that—

(a) if the information or report is not received within the time stipulated by the Commission, it may proceed to inquire into the complaint on its own;

(b) if, on receipt of information or report, the Commission is satisfied either that no further inquiry is required or that the required action has been initiated or taken by the concerned Government or authority, it may not proceed with the complaint and inform the complainant accordingly;

(ii) without prejudice to anything contained in clause (i), if it considers necessary, having regard to the nature of the complaint, initiate an inquiry.

1[18. Steps during and after inquiry.—The Commission may take any of the following steps during or upon the completion of an inquiry held under this Act, namely:— "

(a) where the inquiry discloses the commission of violation of human rights or negligence in the prevention of violation of human rights or abetment thereof by a public servant, it may recommend to the concerned Government or authority—

(i) to make payment of compensation or damages to the complainant or to the victim or the members of his family as the Commission may consider necessary;

(ii) to initiate proceedings for prosecution or such other suitable action as the Commission may deem fit against the concerned person or persons;

(iii) to take such further action as it may think fit.";

(b) approach the Supreme Court or the High Court concerned for such directions, orders or writs as that Court may deem necessary;

(c) recommend to the concerned Government or authority at any stage of the inquiry for the grant of such immediate interim relief to the victim or the members of his family as the Commission may consider necessary;

(d) subject to the provisions of clause (e), provide a copy of the inquiry report to the petitioner or his representative;

(e) the Commission shall send a copy of its inquiry report together with its recommendations to the concerned Government or authority and the concerned Government or authority shall, within a period of one month, or such further time as the Commission may allow, forward its comments on the report, including the action taken or proposed to be taken thereon, to the Commission;

(f) the Commission shall publish its inquiry report together with the comments of the concerned Government or authority, if any, and the action taken or proposed to be taken by the concerned Government or authority on the recommendations of the Commission.]

19. Procedure with respect to armed forces.—
(1) Notwithstanding anything contained in this Act, while dealing with complaints of violation of human rights by members of the armed forces, the Commission shall adopt the following procedure, namely:—

(a) it may, either on its own motion or on receipt of a petition, seek a report from the Central Government;

(b) after the receipt of the report, it may either not proceed with the complaint or, as the case may be, make its recommendations to that Government.

(2) The Central Government shall inform the Commission of the action taken on the recommendations within three months or such further time as the Commission may allow.

(3) The Commission shall publish its report together with its recommendations made to the Central Government and the action taken by that Government on such recommendations.

(4) The Commission shall provide a copy of the report published under sub-section (3) to the petitioner or his representative.

21. Constitution of State Human Rights Commission.—
(1) A State Government may constitute a body to be known as the

.... (Name of the State) Human Rights Commission to exercise the powers conferred upon, and to perform the functions assigned to a State Commission under this Chapter. 1[(2) The State Commission shall, with effect from such date as the State Government may by notification specify, consist of—

(a) a Chairperson who has been a Chief Justice of a High Court;

(b) one Member who is, or has been, a Judge of a High Court or District Judge in the State with a minimum of seven years experience as District Judge;

(c) one Member to be appointed from among persons having knowledge of or practical experience in matters relating to human rights.]

(3) There shall be a Secretary who shall be the Chief Executive Officer of the State Commission and shall exercise such powers and discharge such functions of the State Commission as it may delegate to him.

(4) The headquarters of the State Commission shall be at such place as the State Government may, by notification, specify.

(5) A State Commission may inquire into violation of human rights only in respect of matters relatable to any of the entries enumerated in List II and List III in the Seventh Schedule to the Constitution: Provided that if any such matter is already being inquired into by the Commission or any other Commission duly constituted under any law for the time being in force, the State Commission shall not inquire into the said matter: Provided further that in relation to the Jammu and Kashmir Human Rights Commission, this subsection shall have effect as if for the words and figures "List II and List III in the Seventh Schedule to the Constitution", the words and figures "List III in the Seventh Schedule to the Constitution as applicable to the State of Jammu and Kashmir and in respect of matters in relation to which the Legislature of that State has power to make laws" had been substituted. 2[(6) Two or more State Governments may, with the consent of a Chairperson or Member of a State Commission, appoint such Chairperson or, as the case may be, such Member of another State Commission simultaneously if such

Chairperson or Member consents to such appointment: Provided that every appointment made under this subsection shall be made offer obtaining the recommendations of the committee referred to in sub-section (1) of section 22 in respect of the state for which a common chairman or member, or both, the case may be, is to be appointed.]

29. Application of certain provisions relating to National Human Rights Commission to State Commission.—The provisions of sections 9, 10, 12, 13, 14, 15, 16, 17 and 18 shall apply to a State Commission and shall have effect, subject to the following modifications, namely:—
(a) references to "Commission" shall be construed as references to "State Commission";
(b) in section 10, in sub-section (3), for the words " Secretary-General", the word "Secretary" shall be substituted;
(c) in section 12, clause (f) shall be omitted;
(d) in section 17, in clause (i), the words "Central Government or any" shall be omitted.

30. Human Rights Courts.—For the purpose of providing speedy trial of offences arising out of violation of human rights, the State Government may, with the concurrence of the Chief Justice of the High Court, by notification, specify for each district a Court of Session to be a Human Rights Court to try the said offences: Provided that nothing in this section shall apply if—
(a) a Court of Session is already specified as a special court; or
(b) a special court is already constituted, for such offences under any other law for the time being in force.

31. Special Public Prosecutor.—For every Human Rights Court, the State Government shall, by notification, specify a Public Prosecutor or appoint an advocate who has been in practice as an advocate for not less than seven years, as a Special Public Prosecutor for the purpose of conducting cases in that Court.

32. Grants by the Central Government.—
(1) The Central Government shall, after due appropriation made by Parliament by law in this behalf, pay to the Commission by way of grants such sums of money as the Central Government may think fit for being utilised for the purposes of this Act.
(2) The Commission may spend such sums as it thinks fit for performing the functions under this Act, and such sums shall be treated as expenditure payable out of the grants referred to in sub-section (1).

33. Grants by the State Government.—
(1) The State Government shall, after due appropriation made by Legislature by law in this behalf, pay to the State Commission by way of grants such sums of money as the State Government may think fit for being utilised for the purposes of this Act.
(2) The State Commission may spend such sums as it thinks fit for performing the functions under Chapter V, and such sums shall be treated as expenditure payable out of the grants referred to in sub-section (1).

36. Matters not subject to jurisdiction of the Commission.—
(1) The Commission shall not inquire into any matter which is pending before a State Commission or any other Commission duly constituted under any law for the time being in force.
(2) The Commission or the State Commission shall not inquire into any matter after the expiry of one year from the date on which the act constituting violation of human rights is alleged to have been committed.

37. Constitution of special investigation teams.—Notwithstanding anything contained in any other law for the time being in force, where the Government considers, it necessary so to do, it may constitute one or more special investigation teams, consisting of such police officers as it thinks

necessary for purposes of investigation and prosecution of offences arising out of violations of human rights.

38. Protection of action taken in good faith.—No suit or other legal proceeding shall lie against the Central Government, State Government, Commission, the State Commission or any Member thereof or any person acting under the direction either of the Central Government, State Government, Commission or the State Commission in respect of anything which is in good faith done or intended to be done in pursuance of this Act or of any rules or any order made thereunder or in respect of the publication by or under the authority of the Central Government, State Government, Commission or the State Commission of any report, paper or proceedings.

39. Members and officers to be public servants.—Every Member of the Commission, State Commission and every officer appointed or authorised by the Commission or the State Commission to exercise functions under this Act shall be deemed to be a public servant within the meaning of section 21 of the Indian Penal Code.

40. Power of Central Government to make rules.—

(1) The Central Government may, by notification, make rules to carry out the provisions of this Act.

(2) In particular and without prejudice to the generality of the foregoing power, such rules may provide for all or any of the following matters, namely:—

(a) the salaries and allowances and other terms and conditions of service of the 1[Chairperson and members] under section 8; 1[Chairperson and members] under section 8;"

(b) the conditions subject to which other administrative, technical and scientific staff may be appointed by the Commission and the salaries and allowances of officers and other staff under sub-section (3) of section 11;

(c) any other power of a civil court required to be prescribed under clause (f) of sub-section (1) of section 13;

(d) the form in which the annual statement of accounts is to be prepared by the Commission under sub-section (1) of section 34; and

(e) any other matter which has to be or may be prescribed.

(3) Every rule made under this Act shall be laid, as soon as may be after it is made, before each Houses of Parliament, while it is in session, for a total period of thirty days which may be comprised in one session or in two or more successive sessions, and if, before the expiry of the session immediately following the session or the successive sessions aforesaid, both Houses agree that the rule should not be made, the rule shall thereafter have effect only in such modified form or be of no effect, as the case may be; so, however, that any such modification or annulment shall be without prejudice to the validity of anything previously done under that rule.

26 [40A. Power to make rules retrospectively.—The power to make rules under clause (b) of sub-section (2) of section 40 shall include the power to make such rules or any of them retrospectively from a date not earlier than the date on which this Act received the assent of the President, but no such retrospective effect shall be given to any such rule so as to prejudicially affect the interests of any person to whom such rule may be applicable.]

1[40B. Power of Commission to make regulations.—
(1) Subject to the provisions of this Act and the rules made thereunder, the Commission may, with the previous approval of the Central Government, by notification, make regulations to carry out the provisions of this Act.

(2) In particular and without prejudice to the generality of the foregoing power, such regulations may provide for all or any of the following matters, namely:—
(a) the procedure to be followed by the Commission under sub-

section (2) of section 10;

(b) the returns and statistics to be furnished by the State Commissions;

(c) any other matter which has to be, or may be, specified by regulations.

(3) Every regulation made by the Commission under this Act shall be laid, as soon as may be after it is made, before each House of Parliament, while it is in session, for a total period of thirty days which may be comprised in one session or in two or more successive sessions, and if, before the expiry of the session or the successive sessions aforesaid, both Houses agree in making any modification in the regulation or both Houses agree that the regulation should not be made, the regulation shall thereafter have effect only in such modified form or be of no effect, as the case may be; so, however, that any such modification or annulment shall be without prejudice to the validity of anything previously done under that regulation.]

41. Power of State Government to make rules.—

(1) The State Government may, by notification, make rules to carry out the provisions of this Act.

(2) In particular and without prejudice to the generality of the foregoing power, such rules may provide for all or any of the following matters, namely:—

(a) the salaries and allowances and other terms and conditions of service of 1[the Chairperson and Members] under section 26; 1[the Chairperson and Members] under section 26;"

(b) the conditions subject to which other administrative, technical and scientific staff may be appointed by the State Commission and the salaries and allowances of officers and other staff under sub-section (3) of section 27;

(c) the form in which the annual statement of accounts is to be prepared under sub-section (1) of section 35.

(3) Every rule made by the State Government under this section shall be laid, as soon as may be after it is made, before each House

of the State Legislature where it consists of two Houses, or where such Legislature consists of one House, before that House.

42. Power to remove difficulties.—

(1) If any difficulty arises in giving effect to the provisions of this Act, the Central Government may, by order published in the Official Gazette, make such provisions, not inconsistent with the provisions of this Act as appear to it to be necessary or expedient for removing the difficulty: Provided that no such order shall be made after the expiry of the period of two years from the date of commencement of this Act.

(2) Every order made under this section shall, as soon as may be after it is made, be laid before each House of Parliament.

43. Repeal and savings.—

(1) The Protection of Human Rights Ordinance, 1993 is hereby repealed.

(2) Notwithstanding such repeal, anything done or any action taken under the said Ordinance, shall be deemed to have been done or taken under the corresponding provisions of this Act.

Bibliography

1. Bibliography: DIFFERENCE BETWEEN HUMAN RIGHTS AND FUNDAMENTAL RIGHTS, April 2020, Conference: Human rights education NCHRE-2017At: Alagappa University College of Education, Alagappa University, Karaikudi
Project: Education
Authors:
Prabakaran Balachandran V
GOVERNMENT COLLEGE OF EDUCATION, PUDUKKOTTAI, TAMIL NADU-622001
Dr .AR .Saravanakumar
Alagappa University
2.https://www.youthforhumanrights.org/course/lesson/background-of-human-rights/the-background-of-human-rights.html
3.https://www.ohchr.org/en/professionalinterest/pages/ccpr.aspx
4.http://egyankosh.ac.in//handle/123456789/43221
5.http://egyankosh.ac.in//handle/123456789/43220
6.http://egyankosh.ac.in//handle/123456789/43219
7.http://egyankosh.ac.in//handle/123456789/43218
8. Human Rights; Handbook for Parliamentarians N° 26 - This publication is co-published by the Inter-Parliamentary Union and

the United Nations (Office of the High Commissioner for Human Rights).
9. A Brief Lecture on "HUMAN RIGHTS IN CONSTITUTION OF INDIA" By
DR. ANANT KALSE, PRINCIPAL SECRETARY, MAHARASHTRA LEGISLATURE SECRETARIAT & SECRETARY, COMMONWEALTH PARLIAMENTARY ASSOCIATION, MAHARASHTRA BRANCH Vidhan Bhavan, Mumbai / Nagpur. Venue: UGC - HRDC, 1st Floor, Ranade Bhawan, Vidyanagari

Campus, Kalina, Mumbai. Date: Friday, 30th December 2016 Time: 10.00 A.M. To 11.30 A.M.

¨ MAHARASHTRA LEGISLATURE SECRETARIAT VIDHAN BHAVAN, MUMBAI / NAGPUR.

10. The Protection of Human Rights Act, 1993 ; ACT NO. 10 OF 1994 [8th January 1994.]

Printed by Libri Plureos GmbH in Hamburg,
Germany